FROM TURING TO C...
A BRIEF HISTORY OF AI

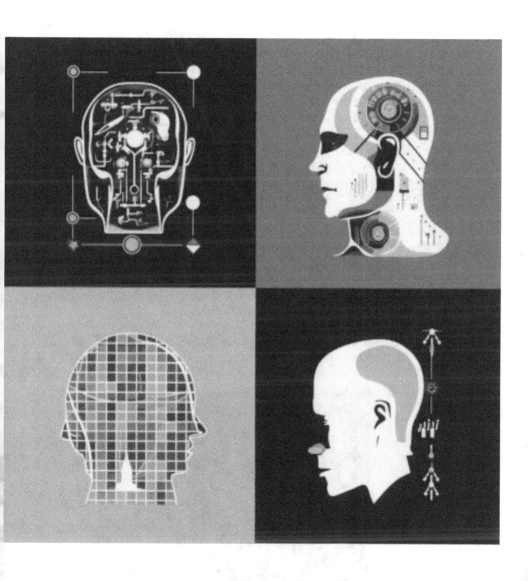

Enlightenment Books

Preface

Artificial intelligence (AI) has become a ubiquitous term in today's world. From virtual assistants to self-driving cars, AI is transforming the way we interact with technology and the world around us. But the history of AI is a long and complex one, spanning more than half a century of research and development.

This book, "From Turing to Chatbots: A Brief History of AI," aims to provide a comprehensive overview of the evolution of AI, from its early beginnings to the modern-day applications we see today. Throughout the book, we will explore the major milestones in AI research and development, the breakthroughs and discoveries that have shaped the field, and the people behind them.

But this is not just a book about the past. We will also examine the current state of AI, including the rise of machine learning, expert systems and robotics, and the use of chatbots in everyday life. Additionally, we will explore the future of AI and the potential it holds for further innovation and advancements.

This book is intended for anyone interested in the fascinating history of AI and its impact on the world around us. Whether you are a student, researcher, or simply curious about the field of AI, this book aims to provide a comprehensive and engaging overview of the history of this rapidly-evolving field.

We hope you enjoy reading "From Turing to Chatbots: A Brief History of AI" as much as we have enjoyed researching and writing it.

Contents

Introduction: The AI Revolution Begins

Imagine a world where machines can learn, reason, and even communicate like humans. A world where intelligent robots are commonplace, and virtual assistants can carry out complex tasks with ease. This is the world of Artificial Intelligence, or AI for short.

AI has been a buzzword for decades, but only recently has it begun to enter our daily lives in meaningful ways. From the self-driving cars on our roads to the personal assistants on our smartphones, AI is rapidly transforming the way we live and work.

But how did we get here? What were the key milestones and breakthroughs that led us to this point? And what does the future hold for AI?

In this book, we will explore the fascinating history of AI, from its early beginnings in the 1950s to the cutting-edge research and applications of today. We will take you on a journey through the key developments in AI, from the birth of expert systems to the rise of machine learning and deep learning.

Along the way, we will meet the pioneers and innovators who shaped the field of AI, from Alan Turing and John McCarthy to Geoffrey Hinton and Demis Hassabis. We will delve into the challenges and controversies that have surrounded AI, from fears of job displacement to concerns about privacy and security.

But this is not just a story of the past. We will also look to the future, exploring the latest trends and breakthroughs in AI, and pondering the ethical and societal implications of these developments. We will ask the tough questions and consider the possibilities, challenging you to think critically and imaginatively about the role of AI in our lives.

So come along on this journey with us, as we explore the thrilling and sometimes frightening world of AI. Whether you're a seasoned expert or a curious newcomer, there's something in this book for you. Together, let's dive into the exciting world of AI and discover what the future holds.

Chapter I: The Origins of AI

It all began in the 1950s, a time of scientific discovery and innovation. In labs across the world, researchers were exploring new frontiers in technology, from nuclear power to space travel. And in the midst of this excitement, a new field of study emerged: Artificial Intelligence, or AI.

The pioneers of AI were an eclectic bunch, from mathematicians and computer scientists to psychologists and linguists. They were united by a common goal: to create machines that could think and reason like humans.

One of the earliest and most influential figures in AI was Alan Turing, a British mathematician and computer scientist. In the 1930s, Turing had laid the groundwork for modern computing with his concept of the Turing machine, a theoretical device that could compute any function that could be computed by a human. But in the 1950s, Turing turned his attention to the question of machine intelligence. He proposed a test, now known as the Turing test, to determine whether a machine could exhibit human-like intelligence. The test involved a human judge communicating with a machine and a human via text, and trying to determine which was the machine. If the judge could not consistently distinguish between the two, the machine would be deemed to have passed the test.

Around the same time, other researchers were working on different approaches to AI. John McCarthy, a computer scientist at Dartmouth College, organized the famous Dartmouth Conference in 1956, which is widely regarded as the birthplace of AI as a formal field of study. At the conference, McCarthy and his colleagues proposed the development of intelligent machines that could perform tasks that normally require human intelligence, such as problem-solving and natural language understanding.

It wasn't until the 1960s and 1970s that AI began to make significant strides. Researchers developed expert systems, which used knowledge-based rules to perform tasks in specialized domains, such as medical diagnosis and engineering. These systems proved to be effective in many applications, but they were limited by their narrow focus and lack of flexibility.

And so the quest for true machine intelligence continued. In the decades that followed, researchers would explore new frontiers in AI, from neural networks and machine learning to deep learning and natural language processing. Each breakthrough would bring us closer to the dream of creating machines that can think, learn, and reason like humans.

But the journey would not be without its challenges and setbacks. As we will explore in the coming chapters, AI has faced criticism and controversy, from fears of job displacement to concerns about the ethical and social implications of intelligent machines.

But for now, let us marvel at the pioneers of AI and their audacious dreams. Let us appreciate the ingenuity and perseverance that has brought us to this point. And let us wonder at the possibilities that lie ahead.

Chapter II: AI Breakthroughs and Milestones

It's time to fasten your seatbelt because we're going on a wild ride through the history of AI breakthroughs and milestones! From chess champions to self-driving cars, AI has made some incredible achievements over the years. So let's buckle up and take a trip down memory lane.

One of the earliest breakthroughs in AI was the creation of the General Problem Solver (GPS) in the 1950s. Developed by Herbert Simon and Allen Newell, two pioneers of AI, GPS was a computer program that could solve a wide range of problems by breaking them down into smaller sub-problems. It was a major milestone in the development of AI, demonstrating the potential for machines to tackle complex tasks.

In the 1990s, AI made a big splash in the world of chess when IBM's Deep Blue defeated world champion Garry Kasparov. The victory was a major milestone in AI, showing that machines could beat humans at one of the most complex games ever invented.

But AI wasn't just making waves in the world of games. In the early 2000s, a team of researchers led by Geoffrey Hinton developed deep learning, a technique for training neural networks to recognize patterns in data. This breakthrough revolutionized computer vision and speech recognition, allowing machines to recognize objects in images and understand human speech with greater accuracy than ever before.

In 2011, IBM's Watson made headlines by defeating two of the greatest Jeopardy! champions of all time. Watson was a natural language processing system that could understand and respond to complex questions in English. Its victory was a major breakthrough in AI, demonstrating the potential for machines to understand and process natural language.

In the years that followed, AI continued to make incredible strides. Self-driving cars became a reality, thanks to advances in machine learning and computer vision. Robots began to take over dangerous jobs, from defusing bombs to exploring space. And AI-powered assistants, like Siri and Alexa, became commonplace in homes and offices around the world.

But the journey hasn't been without its challenges. AI has faced criticism and skepticism, with concerns about job displacement and ethical implications. However, the potential benefits of AI are vast, from improving healthcare and education to revolutionizing transportation and energy.

So let's keep exploring and pushing the boundaries of what machines can do. The future of AI is bright, and who knows what incredible breakthroughs and milestones are waiting just around the corner.

Chapter III: The Rise of Machine Learning

Get ready to dive into the exciting world of machine learning! This is the technology that's driving some of the biggest breakthroughs in AI today, from personalized recommendations to self-driving cars.

At the heart of machine learning is the idea of training algorithms to recognize patterns in data. It's a bit like teaching a baby to recognize different animals - you show them pictures of dogs, cats, and birds, and over time they learn to recognize each one.

The same principle applies to machine learning. We feed algorithms lots of data, like images or text, and they learn to recognize patterns in that data. For example, if we show an algorithm thousands of pictures of cats, it will eventually learn to recognize what a cat looks like.

One of the most exciting applications of machine learning is in the field of computer vision. This is the technology that allows machines to "see" and understand images. Thanks to advances in machine learning, computers can now recognize objects in images with incredible accuracy, even outperforming humans in some cases!

Another area where machine learning is making a big impact is in natural language processing (NLP). This is the technology that allows machines to understand and interpret human language. Thanks to machine learning, NLP systems can now understand the nuances of human speech and even generate human-like responses.

But perhaps the most exciting application of machine learning is in self-driving cars. These vehicles use complex algorithms and sensors to navigate roads and avoid obstacles. By training these algorithms on vast amounts of driving data, engineers have been able to create cars that can drive themselves with remarkable precision.

Of course, machine learning isn't without its challenges. One of the biggest issues is the need for vast amounts of data to train these algorithms. In some cases, this data can be hard to come by or may be biased in ways that can affect the accuracy of the algorithms.

Despite these challenges, the rise of machine learning has opened up incredible new possibilities for AI. From personalized recommendations to self-driving cars, the potential for this technology is truly limitless. So buckle up and get ready for an exciting ride into the world of machine learning!

Chapter IV: Expert Systems & Robotics

Are you ready to meet some of the smartest machines out there? In this chapter, we'll dive into the world of expert systems and robotics - the technologies that are revolutionizing industries from healthcare to manufacturing.

Expert systems are a type of AI that specializes in solving complex problems by mimicking the decision-making processes of human experts. These systems use "if-then" rules to analyze data and make decisions, just like a human expert would. For example, a medical expert system might use data from a patient's symptoms to diagnose a disease.

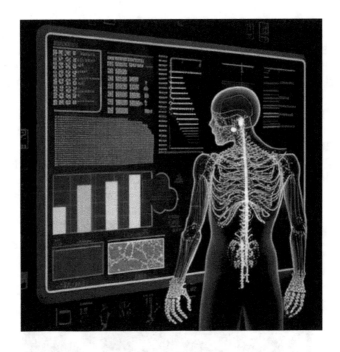

Another type of smart machine that's making waves in industries all over the world is robotics. These are machines that can perform physical tasks autonomously, like assembling cars or packaging products.

One of the most exciting applications of robotics is in healthcare. For example, surgical robots can perform minimally invasive surgeries with incredible precision, reducing recovery times and improving patient outcomes.

Another field where robotics is having a big impact is in manufacturing. Robots can perform repetitive tasks with incredible accuracy and speed, helping companies increase efficiency and reduce costs.

But perhaps the most exciting aspect of expert systems and robotics is their potential for collaboration. By combining the strengths of human experts with the precision and speed of machines, we can create systems that are more efficient, accurate, and effective than either could be on their own.

Of course, there are also challenges that come with these technologies. For example, ensuring the safety and ethical use of autonomous machines is an ongoing concern. But as we continue to develop and refine these technologies, the potential for expert systems and robotics to transform our world is truly limitless.

So get ready to meet some of the smartest machines out there and discover the amazing ways they're changing our world!

Chapter V: AI in the Modern Era

Welcome to the world of modern AI! In this chapter, we'll explore some of the coolest, most cutting-edge AI technologies that are changing the way we live, work, and play.

One of the most exciting things about modern AI is its ability to learn from vast amounts of data. This is known as advanced machine learning, and it's the technology behind many of the most impressive AI systems we have today.

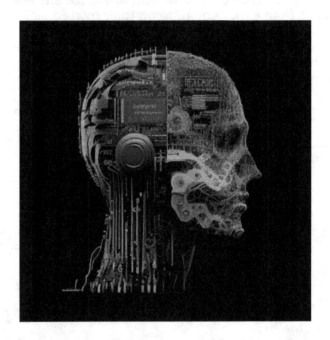

For example, advanced machine learning is what powers voice assistants like Siri and Alexa, which can understand natural language and respond to our requests in real-time. It's also what's behind self-driving cars, which use sensors and AI algorithms to navigate our roads and avoid accidents.

But advanced machine learning is just the tip of the iceberg when it comes to modern AI. Another technology that's gaining traction is deep learning, which involves training neural networks - a type of AI architecture inspired by the human brain - to perform complex tasks like image recognition and natural language processing.

Thanks to deep learning, we now have AI systems that can identify objects in photos with incredible accuracy, and even generate realistic images and videos from scratch. And with natural language processing, we're starting to see AI systems that can understand and respond to human language in more sophisticated ways than ever before.

Of course, there are also challenges and concerns that come with these technologies, such as the potential for bias and the need to protect data privacy. But as we continue to develop and refine AI in the modern era, the potential for innovation and transformation is truly staggering.

So get ready to dive into the exciting world of modern AI and discover the cutting-edge technologies that are changing our world in ways we never thought possible!

Chapter VI: ChatGPT and Other Chatbots

Have you ever chatted with a robot? In this chapter, we'll explore the fascinating world of chatbots, including the one and only Chat GPT!

Chatbots are AI systems that can communicate with people through text or voice, just like a human would. They can answer questions, make recommendations, and even have conversations with us.

Chat GPT is one of the most impressive chatbots out there, thanks to its ability to generate human-like responses to any given prompt. It uses advanced natural language processing and machine learning algorithms to understand what we're saying and generate a response that's both relevant and engaging.

But Chat GPT is just the beginning when it comes to chatbots. There are countless other chatbots out there, each with its own unique personality and set of skills. For example, there are chatbots that can help you order pizza, book a hotel room, or even provide mental health support.

One of the most exciting things about chatbots is their potential for improving customer service. By providing 24/7 support and personalized recommendations, chatbots can help companies save money and improve customer satisfaction.

Of course, there are also concerns about the use of chatbots, such as the potential for biased responses or the need for transparency around how data is being used. But as chatbot technology continues to evolve, we're sure to see even more impressive and useful applications.

So get ready to meet Chat GPT and other fascinating chatbots, and discover the amazing ways they're changing the way we communicate with machines!

Chapter VII: AI and Ethics - Navigating the Moral Maze

As we venture into the world of AI, it's important to remember that with great power comes great responsibility. AI has the potential to revolutionize industries and improve lives, but it's also important to consider the ethical implications.

Imagine a world where AI makes all the decisions, from who gets hired for a job to who receives medical treatment. Sounds like something out of a sci-fi movie, right? Well, this could become a reality if we don't navigate the ethical maze carefully.

AI has the potential to reinforce biases and perpetuate discrimination, whether intentional or not. For example, a hiring algorithm could inadvertently discriminate against women or people of color if it's trained on biased data. It's up to us to ensure that the data sets used to train AI systems are diverse and inclusive.

Chapter VII: AI and Ethics - Navigating the Moral Maze

In addition, there's the issue of transparency. AI algorithms are often considered black boxes, meaning that it's difficult to understand how they arrived at a certain decision. This lack of transparency can make it challenging to identify and address ethical issues.

Another consideration is the impact of AI on jobs. As AI becomes more advanced, there's the possibility that it could replace jobs traditionally done by humans. It's important to consider how we can ensure a fair transition for workers as industries shift towards AI.

Ultimately, it's up to us to make ethical considerations a priority as we continue to develop and implement AI. By doing so, we can ensure that the benefits of AI are shared equitably and that we don't inadvertently create a world that we don't want to live in.

Chapter VIII: AI's Impact on Society & Work

Artificial Intelligence (AI) has the potential to revolutionize the way we live and work. As we continue to develop more advanced AI technologies, it's important to consider the impact they may have on our society and the future of work.

One major concern is the displacement of jobs. As AI becomes more sophisticated, it has the ability to perform tasks previously done by humans, leading to job losses in some industries. However, many experts believe that AI will also create new job opportunities, particularly in fields related to AI development and maintenance.

Another potential impact of AI on society is the ethical and social implications. As AI becomes more ubiquitous, there are concerns about the misuse of AI, including the potential for biased decision-making and the erosion of privacy. It's important for developers and policymakers to consider these issues and implement appropriate safeguards to ensure the responsible use of AI.

Chapter VIII: AI and Ethics - AI's Impact on Society & Work

Despite these concerns, there are also many positive impacts of AI on society. AI has the potential to improve healthcare outcomes, increase efficiency in industries like manufacturing and transportation, and even aid in disaster response efforts.

Additionally, AI has the potential to level the playing field by providing access to information and resources to people who may have previously been disadvantaged.

As we continue to develop and integrate AI into our society, it's important to consider both the potential benefits and risks. By working together to address these concerns, we can ensure that AI is used to improve our lives in a responsible and ethical way.

Chapter IX: The Future of AI

Are you ready to imagine the future? In this chapter, we'll take a look at some of the most exciting possibilities for AI in the years and decades to come.

One of the biggest areas of growth for AI is in the field of healthcare. Imagine a world where doctors have access to AI systems that can analyze patient data and identify diseases with unprecedented accuracy. This could lead to faster, more effective treatments and even cures for some of the most challenging diseases.

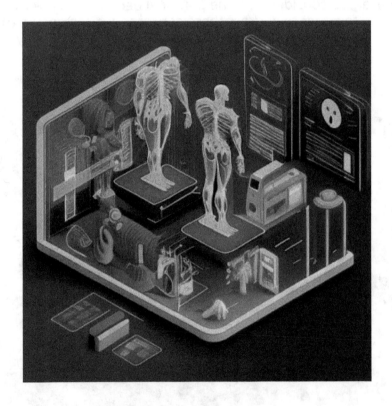

AI also has the potential to revolutionize transportation. Self-driving cars are just the beginning - imagine a future where traffic flow is optimized in real-time, reducing congestion and saving time for everyone on the road. Or how about a world where drones and delivery robots work together to make same-day delivery a reality for everyone?

Another exciting possibility for AI is in the field of entertainment. With the help of AI algorithms, we could soon have fully interactive, personalized experiences in video games, movies, and even theme parks. Imagine a game that can adapt to your play style, or a movie that changes based on your emotions and reactions.

But with all these exciting possibilities also come some concerns. How do we ensure that AI is used ethically and responsibly? How do we protect our privacy and data in a world where machines are constantly learning about us?

These are big questions, but as we look to the future of AI, it's important to keep them in mind. With careful planning and responsible development, we can unlock the full potential of this incredible technology and create a future that's both exciting and sustainable.

So get ready to dream big, and imagine the amazing things we could accomplish with AI in the years and decades to come!

Chapter X: Conclusion

Congratulations, you've made it to the end of our journey through the history of AI! We hope you've enjoyed learning about the incredible breakthroughs, milestones, and possibilities of this amazing technology.

As we've seen, AI has come a long way since its earliest days, and we're now living in a world where it's hard to imagine life without it. From self-driving cars to voice assistants, AI is all around us, making our lives easier and more efficient.

But as we look to the future, it's important to remember that AI is still a rapidly-evolving technology. There are still many questions to be answered, and many challenges to be overcome.

But with the right approach, we can ensure that AI continues to be a force for good in the world. By focusing on responsible development, ethical use, and collaboration between humans and machines, we can create a future that's both exciting and sustainable.

So what's next for AI? Well, that's up to you! With your imagination and creativity, the possibilities are endless. So keep dreaming, keep innovating, and keep pushing the boundaries of what's possible.

Thanks for joining us on this journey, and we can't wait to see what the future holds for AI!